BUZZING WITH QUESTIONS

The Inquisitive Mind of Charles Henry Turner

JANICE N. HARRINGTON

Illustrated by
THEODORE TAYLOR III

CALKINS CREEK
AN IMPRINT OF BOYDS MILLS & KANE
New York

To my agent, Stephen Fraser: Thank you!
And to RDP always.
—JNH

To my son Theo.
Never stop exploring!
—TTIII

"The study of biology trains the powers of observation."

—Charles Henry Turner

Questions that itched like mosquito bites, questions that tickled like spider webs, questions you just couldn't shoo away! Questions hopped through Charles Henry Turner's mind like grasshoppers. His brain buzzed with questions about plants and animals and bugs.

His parents' home swarmed with books, but never enough books to answer all his questions. Charles Henry Turner asked so many questions that his teacher urged him to "go and find out." And Charles did.

He read and studied and worked hard. And after he finished
high school, he did what many people thought impossible:
    even though he was a janitor's son,
    even though most colleges didn't accept African American
        students,
    even though it meant more hard work,
    Charles Henry Turner went to college.

In his biology class, Charles met the magnetic young teacher Clarence L. Herrick. Herrick's classes hummed with energy: students chatting, students examining the organs of small animals, and students staring one-eyed through microscopes.

On Friday afternoons, Herrick invited students to his laboratory for spirited talks about biology. He spread tablecloths over the long laboratory tables and set out sweet cakes and cups of tea. But Herrick worried about inviting Charles Henry Turner.

He worried that the other students wouldn't want to drink tea with his only brown-skinned student. To Herrick's delight, the other students wanted Charles to join them. They liked the shy, quiet student who always earned high grades, the hardworking Charles Henry Turner.

Charles was "indefatigable," a classmate said. He spent hours peering through microscopes, planning experiments, gathering specimens, keeping records, drawing charts, and reading scientific papers in French and German. But whatever the language, he never stopped asking questions.

One question led Charles to a small, eight-legged, eight-eyed, two-fanged creature: the spider. Charles wanted to know if spiders could learn or if they were only weaving machines that made the same web over and over.

Charles searched for spider webs. He trudged through meadows, inspected stone walls, and scouted the sides of railroad tracks. He toppled woodpiles, lingered over logs, and peeked into dusty corners. Charles found webs, lots of them. He even spotted double webs that looked, he wrote, as if the spider were trying "to fish with two lines instead of one."

All kinds of spiders and all kinds of webs caught Charles's attention, even a web between a windowsill and a wall. What would the spider do, Charles wondered, if he swept away its web?

With a broom, Charles brushed away the web. Not knowing it was part of a science experiment, the unsuspecting spider rebuilt its web. Sweep away. Rebuild. Sweep away. Rebuild. After losing its web for the fifth time, the spider gave up and wove a new home beneath the windowsill.

But Charles didn't give up.

He repeated his experiment with an arachnarium, a spider jar. He filled the bottom of the jar with sand and pushed a post into the sand. Then he added a spider. He slipped a paper triangle into the jar and watched the spider. Later, he removed the paper triangle, replaced it with an L-shaped tube, and watched again. With each change, the spider rewove and reshaped its web. Charles concluded that instinct told spiders to make their webs, but that each spider wove a web just right for its home. Charles called this "intelligent action."

Spiders were not just weaving machines.

The indefatigable scientist then wondered about even smaller animals. In scummy ponds and weedy ditches, he searched for tiny crustaceans. He found seed shrimp, water fleas, and wheel animals. Through his microscope, he admired their small bodies. They were "beautiful" and "translucent," and some looked like "a nest of test tubes." Charles even discovered a new crustacean and named it *Cypris herricki,* after his friend and teacher Clarence L. Herrick.

But Charles didn't, couldn't, wouldn't stop asking questions. At thirty-nine, he returned to school. He wanted to learn. He wanted to ask BIG questions about another small creature: the ant.

Charles wondered how ants found their way home. Did ants have a hidden power in their brains that pulled them to their nests? Did the sun guide them? Did they follow a trail of smells?

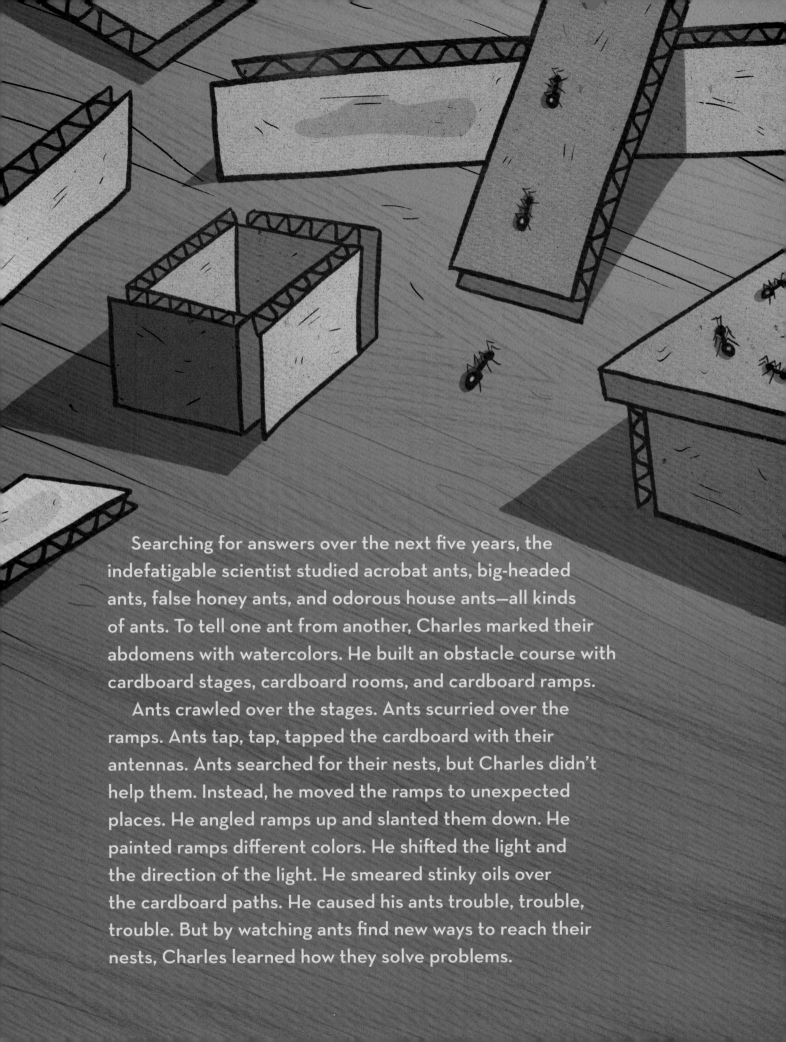

Searching for answers over the next five years, the indefatigable scientist studied acrobat ants, big-headed ants, false honey ants, and odorous house ants—all kinds of ants. To tell one ant from another, Charles marked their abdomens with watercolors. He built an obstacle course with cardboard stages, cardboard rooms, and cardboard ramps.

Ants crawled over the stages. Ants scurried over the ramps. Ants tap, tap, tapped the cardboard with their antennas. Ants searched for their nests, but Charles didn't help them. Instead, he moved the ramps to unexpected places. He angled ramps up and slanted them down. He painted ramps different colors. He shifted the light and the direction of the light. He smeared stinky oils over the cardboard paths. He caused his ants trouble, trouble, trouble. But by watching ants find new ways to reach their nests, Charles learned how they solve problems.

Charles drew a map with squiggly lines and arrows to show the wandering path of a lost ant. A French scientist called this wandering *Tournoiement de Turner* or "Turner's circling," in honor of Charles Henry Turner, the scientist who taught us that ants were not mindless robots. Each ant used sight, sound, touch, smell, the movement of its body, and sunlight to find its way home.

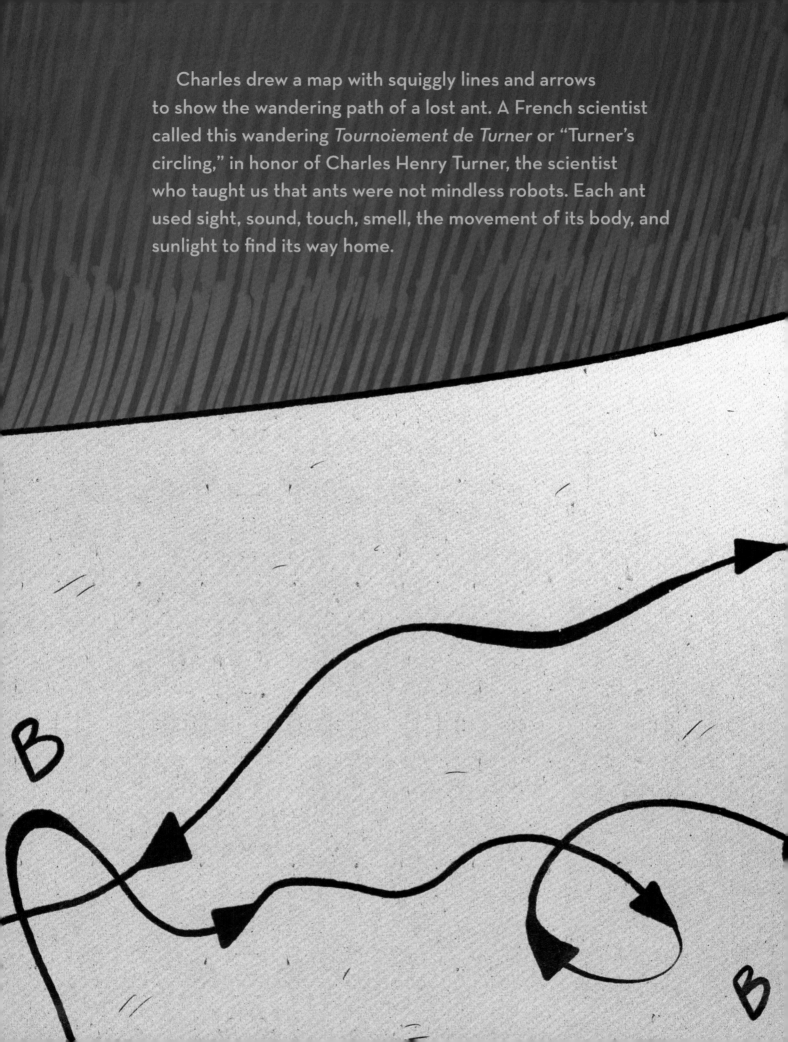

Like the ants, Charles now searched for a new home. He found work as a biology teacher at the first African American high school west of the Mississippi—Sumner High School in St. Louis.

Excited by their new teacher, students filled their lab books with notes about his class. One student wrote that Charles set out dishes of jam for bees at breakfast, lunch, and dinner. The bees circled and buzzed at each meal. But then when Charles set out jam only at breakfast, the bees still invited themselves to lunch and dinner. Surprised, the students learned that even bees sense time.

Questions kept circling and buzzing in Charles's mind.
In a St. Louis park, the scientist placed red cardboard circles
in a patch of clover that swarmed with bees. He coated the
circles with honey, and then he waited. The bees weren't
interested in his circles. They weren't even drawn to the
smell of honey.

But good scientists are patient, so Charles tried again.

He caught bees in a bottle and toppled them over the honey. At first the bees buzzed away, but eventually they settled on the cardboard to enjoy a sip of honey. Once the bees learned that the red circles carried honey, Charles replaced the red circles with honey-filled blue circles. The bees (*bzzzz*) ignored them.

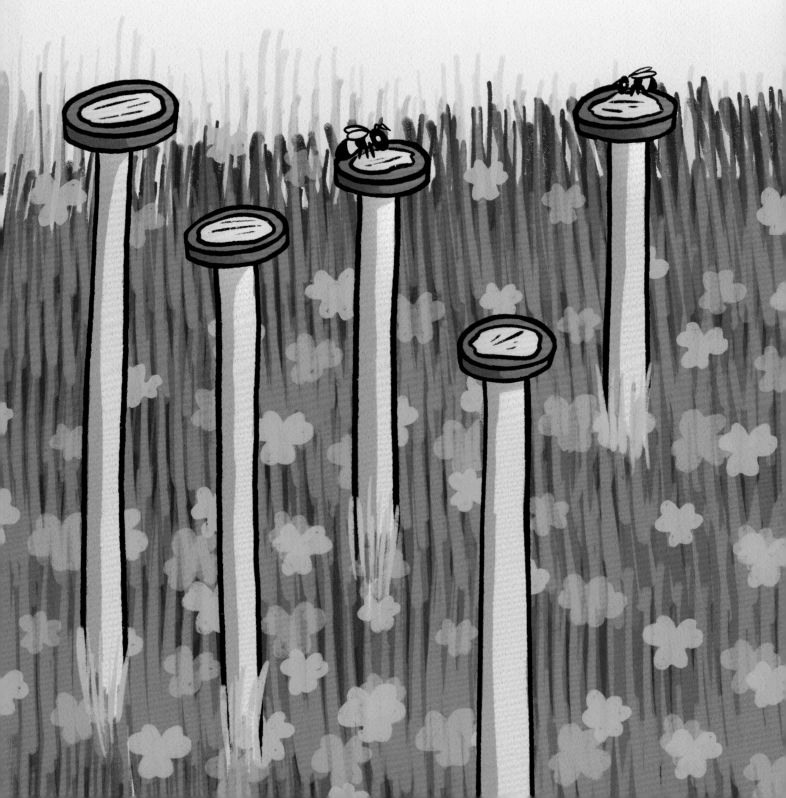

Whether he used circles or cones or boxes or added new colors, the bees kept flying to the color red, even when another color held lots of honey. In thirty-two different experiments (*bzzzzz*), no matter how Charles tried to trick them (*bzzz*), the bees chose the color red. Charles Henry Turner (*bzzzz*) was the first biologist to prove scientifically that bees could see color.

Bees, giant water bugs, whirligig beetles, dragonfly nymphs, water striders, paper wasps, hornets, or tent caterpillars, Charles studied them all.

He taught cockroaches to find their way through a maze, proving that they could learn.

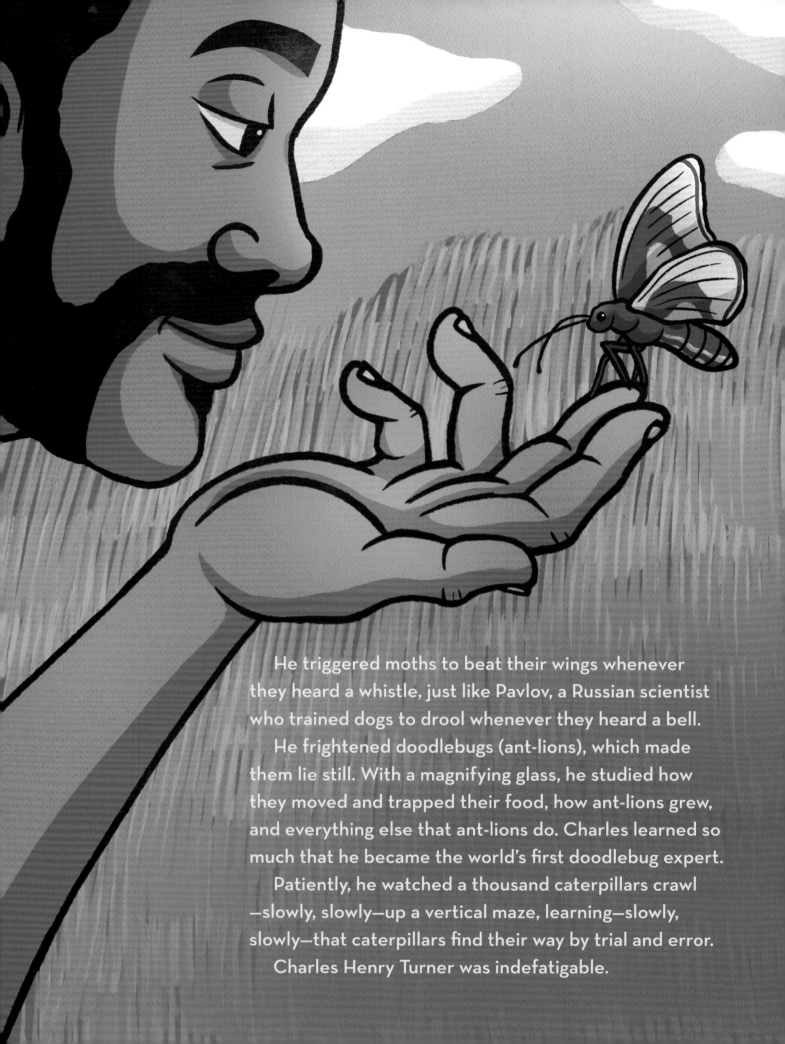

He triggered moths to beat their wings whenever they heard a whistle, just like Pavlov, a Russian scientist who trained dogs to drool whenever they heard a bell.

He frightened doodlebugs (ant-lions), which made them lie still. With a magnifying glass, he studied how they moved and trapped their food, how ant-lions grew, and everything else that ant-lions do. Charles learned so much that he became the world's first doodlebug expert.

Patiently, he watched a thousand caterpillars crawl —slowly, slowly—up a vertical maze, learning—slowly, slowly—that caterpillars find their way by trial and error. Charles Henry Turner was indefatigable.

His mazes, spider jars, paper circles, and cardboard stages toppled old ideas about insects. He never stopped inventing new ways to study the smallest creatures, searching for new ideas, or asking new questions.

Questions that itched like mosquito bites, questions that tickled like spider webs, questions that only a good experiment could shoo away!

As hardworking as the ants and bees he studied, Charles published over fifty scientific papers on everything from bird brains and the bathroom habits of cockroaches to blind crayfish and the growth of grape leaves. He was a pioneer scientist of animal behavior, an internationally admired entomologist, and one of the leading African American scientists of his time.

But even though he was a respected scientist, Charles faced racial prejudice. He lived in the South, where African Americans had to attend separate schools, and where they could rarely vote. He lived in St. Louis when the terrible East St. Louis Race Riot erupted across the Mississippi River. Hateful mobs killed more than a hundred African Americans and burned their neighborhoods.

Yet despite this prejudice, Charles wove himself into his community. He raised money for poor families and led a settlement house that sold lunches to hungry children for only a penny. He worked with white and black people to make St. Louis a better place for everybody.

Biology—the study of plants and animals—gave Charles hope. He wrote that biology could help people see the connections among all living things. Biology taught us to think less about ourselves and more about others.

Charles Henry Turner, the boy who never stopped asking questions, grew into the tireless reader who owned a thousand books. He was the good friend always willing to help other scientists by offering ideas, helping with research, or sharing his equipment. "If my micro-camera proves a success, I shall be glad for you to use it whenever you desire."

Charles Henry Turner, the boy who never stopped asking questions, grew into the determined biologist who would stay up all night to watch a spider or spend all day observing wasps beside a railroad track. "I shall take my camera along and get a few photographs."

His curiosity danced from experiment to experiment.

It moved in Turner's circles, in *Tournoiement de Turner*, always exploring, always reaching to discover new ideas.

Charles Henry Turner, the boy whose teacher urged him "to go and find out," grew into a teacher himself, a devoted scholar who taught students to look closely, to find the webs that connect us all, and—just as he did—to fill the world with questions, questions, questions.

> "Often I have failed, my patience
> not being a match for the persistence of the ant;
> in other cases, by patient persistence,
> I have succeeded."
> —Charles Henry Turner

AUTHOR'S NOTE

When I was young, my uncles would bring me a "june bug helicopter" every summer, a rainbow-shiny beetle tied to a cotton string. The june bug would fly in a circle at the end of the string. When the june bug tired out, I untied it and let it fly away. Maybe that's why the book *Bug Watching with Charles Henry Turner* by Michael Elsohn Ross caught my attention. As a children's librarian and an African American, I was surprised that I had never heard of Charles Henry Turner. He was a mystery, and I wanted to know more. Thanks to the African American newspapers of the time, the work of scholars such as Charles I. Abramson, and the libraries, archives, and historical museums in St. Louis, Kansas City, and Cincinnati, I slowly answered some of my questions. I felt drawn to Turner's indefatigable passion for learning. He studied so many topics that some scientists call him an entomologist or zoologist, while others call him a comparative biologist or a behavioral psychologist.

Turner also lived in my home state of Illinois, attending college in Chicago and studying a colony of wasps in Lebanon, Illinois, where he wrote, after watching a wasp find its way home, "How keen . . . must be her powers of observation since she sees landmarks in a situation where we see only uniformity!" Turner believed that biology helps us to see—to look at the world more closely. In these times when so many animals, insects, and plants are endangered or disappearing, what could be a more vital gift? Look at the world. Ask questions. Search for new answers.

Prof. C. H. Turner

"There is much evidence that the responses
of moths to stimuli are expressions of emotion.
The fact that an insect does not respond to a sound
is no sign that it does not hear it.
The response depends upon whether or not
the sound has a life significance."
—Charles Henry Turner

TIMELINE*

1867	Charles Henry Turner born to Thomas Turner and Adeline Campbell Turner, February 3, in Cincinnati, Ohio. His father worked as a janitor and his mother as a practical nurse. By 1880, Charles had two younger sisters.
1886	Enrolls as a student at the University of Cincinnati.
1887	Marries Leontine Troy.
1888–1889	Teacher at Governor Street School in Evansville, Indiana.
1890	Birth of Turner's daughter Louisa Mae.
1891	Awarded Bachelor of Science from the University of Cincinnati.
1891	Birth of Turner's son Henry Owen.
1891–1892	Assistant teacher in the Biological Laboratory for the University of Cincinnati.
1892	Receives a Master of Science degree. He is the first African American to receive a graduate degree at the University of Cincinnati.
1892–1905	Professor of Biology and Department Head of Science and Agriculture at Clark University, a school for African Americans in Atlanta, Georgia.
1894	Birth of Turner's son Darwin Romanes.
1895	Leontine Turner dies.
1905–1906	Principal of College Hill School in Cleveland, Tennessee.
1907	Awarded PhD in zoology from the University of Chicago, magna cum laude.
1907 or 1908	Marries Lillian Porter.
1907–1908	Teaches at Haines Normal and Industrial Institute in Augusta, Georgia.
1908	Begins teaching biology at Sumner High School in St. Louis, Missouri.
1910	Victor Cornetz, a French naturalist, names the circling of ants "*Tournoiement de Turner.*"
1910	The first African American scientist admitted to the St. Louis Academy of Science.
1922	Retires from Sumner High School.
1923	Dies February 14 in Chicago, Illinois.
1925	St. Louis school board names the Charles Henry Turner Open Air School for Crippled Children after Turner. It is now the Turner Middle School.

* Historians disagree about certain dates in Turner's life and there are no accurate records.

SOURCES

1880 United States Federal Census. Census Place: *Cincinnati, Hamilton, Ohio*; Roll: 1024; Family History Film: 1255024; page 103A; Enumeration District: 113; Image: 0066.

Abramson, Charles I. "A Study in Inspiration: Charles Henry Turner (1867-1923) and the Investigation of Insect Behavior." *Annual Review of Entomology* 54.1 (2009): 343-59.

Barnes, Harper. *Never Been a Time: The 1917 Race Riot that Sparked the Civil Rights Movement.* New York: Walker, 2008.

Bouvier, E. L. *The Psychic Life of Insects.* Translated by L. O. Howard. New York: Century, 1922.

Bowles, Carrie K. "Social Work Among Colored People in St. Louis." *Opportunity: Journal of Negro Life* 14.9 (Sept. 1936): 280-282.

Cadwallader, Thomas C. "Neglected Aspects of the Evolution of American Comparative and Animal Psychology." *Behavioral Evolution and Integrative Levels.* Edited by Gary Greenberg and Ethel Tobach. Hillsdale, NJ: Lawrence Erlbaum, 1984. 15-48.

Chessman, G. Wallace. *Denison: The Story of an Ohio College.* Granville, Ohio: Denison University, 1957.

Coghill, G. E. "Clarence Luther Herrick as Teacher and Friend." *Journal of Comparative Neurology* 74.1 (Feb. 1941): 39-42.

Cornetz, Victor. "Trajets de fourmis et retours au nid." *Mémoires Institut Général Psychologique* 2 (1910): 1-167.

Dewsbury, Donald A., "Foreword." *Selected Papers and Biography.*

Ferguson, Edward Jr. "A Revised List of Papers Published by Charles Henry Turner." *Journal of Negro Education* 9.4 (1940): 657-60.

Haines, D. E. "The Contributors to Volume 1 (1891) of *The Journal of Comparative Neurology. . . .*" *Journal of Comparative Neurology* 314.1 (1991): 9-33.

Hayden, Robert C. *Seven Black American Scientists.* Reading, MA: Addison-Wesley, 1970.

Herrick, Charles Judson. "Clarence Luther Herrick: Pioneer Naturalist, Teacher, and Psychobiologist." *Transactions of the American Philosophical Society*, New Series, 45.1 (1955): 1-85.

McKissack, Patricia and Fredrick. *African-American Scientists.* Brookfield, CT: Millbrook Press, 1994.

"Personal and General." *Southwestern Christian Advocate* 27 (July 7, 1898): 9.

"Prof. Charles Henry Turner, M. S." *Twentieth Century Negro Literature.* Edited by Daniel Wallace Culp. Naperville, IL: J. L. Nichols, 1902. Between pages 162 and 163.

Rau, Phil. "The Scientific Work of Dr. Charles Henry Turner." *Transactions of the Academy of Science of St. Louis* 24.9 (Dec. 1923): 10-16.

Ross, Michael Elsohn. *Bug Watching with Charles Henry Turner*. Minneapolis: Carolrhoda Books, 1997.

Selected Papers and Biography of Charles Henry Turner (1867-1923). Edited by Charles I. Abramson, Camille L. Fuller, and Latasha D. Jackson. Lewiston, NY: Edwin Mellen Press, 2003.

Simpson, Gordon H. Letter to W.E.B. Du Bois. Dec. 26, 1923. W.E.B. Du Bois Papers, 1803–1999. Special Collections and University Archives, University of Massachusetts Amherst Libraries.

Sumner High School. "Charles Henry Turner (1867-1922)." *The Maroon and White* 5, 1924. St. Louis: St. Louis Public Schools, 1924. 60. Reprinted in *Biographical Sketches of St. Louisans*. St. Louis: St. Louis Public Library, 1996.

Tight, W. G. "Clarence Luther Herrick." *American Geologist* 36.1 (July 1905): 1–26.

Turner, C. H. Letters to Phil Rau. Edwin P. Meiners Collection. Folder 195. State Historical Society of Missouri.

Who's Who of the Colored Race: A General Biographical Dictionary of Men and Women of African Descent. Vol. 1. Edited by Frank Lincoln Mather. Chicago, 1915. 267–268.

Windle, William Frederick. *The Pioneering Role of Clarence Luther Herrick in American Neuroscience*. Hicksville, NY: Exposition Press, 1979.

WEBSITE

The Charles Henry Turner Webpage: psychology.okstate.edu/museum/turner/turnermain.html

SELECTED PAPERS BY CHARLES HENRY TURNER

"Experiments on Color-Vision of the Honey Bee." *Biological Bulletin* 19.5 (Oct. 1910): 257–79.

"Experiments on Pattern-Vision of the Honey Bee." *Biological Bulletin* 21.5 (Oct. 1911): 249–64.

"An Experimental Study of the Auditory Powers of the Giant Silkworm Moths (Saturniidae)." *Biological Bulletin* 27.6 (Dec. 1914): 325–32.

"The Homing of Ants: An Experimental Study of Ant Behavior." Dissertation. University of Chicago, 1907.

"The Homing of Ants: An Experimental Study of Ant Behavior." *Journal of Comparative Neurology and Psychology* 17.5 (Sept. 1907): 367–434.

"Morphology of the Avian Brains." *Journal of Comparative Neurology* 1.1 (1891): 39–92, 107–33, 265–86.

"Notes on the Behavior of the Ant-Lion with Emphasis on the Feeding Activities and Letisimulation." *Biological Bulletin* 29.5 (1915): 277–307.

"Notes upon the Cladocera, Copepoda, Ostracoda, and Rotifera, of Cincinnati, with Description of New Species." *Bulletin of the Scientific Laboratories of Denison University* 6.2 (1892): 57–74.

"Psychological Notes upon the Gallery Spider—Illustrations of Intelligent Variations in the Construction of the Web." *Journal of Comparative Neurology* 2.1 (1892): 95–110.

"Reasons for Teaching the Negro Biology." *Southwestern Christian Advocate* 32.14 (1897): 2.

"Recent Researches on the Behavior of the Higher Invertebrates." *Psychological Bulletin* 5.6 (June 1908): 190–95.

"The Sun-Dance of Melissodes." *Psyche* 15 (Dec. 1908): 122–24.

"A Week with a Mining Eumenid: An Ecologico Behavior Study of the Nesting Habits of *Odynerus dorsalis* Fab." *Biological Bulletin* 42.4 (Apr. 1922): 153–72.

"Will the Education of the Negro Solve the Race Problem?" *Twentieth Century Negro Literature.* Edited by Daniel Wallace Culp. Naperville, IL: J. L. Nichols, 1902. 162–66.

NOTES

Page 3: "The study of biology . . .": Turner, "Reasons for Teaching the Negro Biology."

Page 5: "go and find out . . .": Hayden, p. 70.

Page 10: "indefatigable": Herrick, p. 37.

Page 13: "to fish with two . . .": Turner, "Psychological Notes upon the Gallery Spider," p. 101.

Page 15: "intelligent action": Ibid., p. 110.

Page 16–17: "beautiful": Turner, "Notes upon the Cladocera," p. 59.

Page 16–17: "translucent": Turner, "Notes upon the Cladocera," p. 66.

Page 16–17: "a nest of test tubes": Turner, "Notes upon the Cladocera," p. 71.

Page 22: "Turner's circling": Cornetz, p. 270.

Page 36–37: "If my micro-camera . . .": Letter to Phil Rau, July 26, 1915.

Page 38–39: "I shall take . . .": Letter to Phil Rau, July 26, 1915.

Page 40–41: "to go and find out . . .": Hayden, p. 70.

Page 42: "How keen . . .": Turner, "A Week with a Mining Eumenid," p. 163.

Page 42: "Often I have failed . . .": Turner, "The Homing of Ants," p. 387.

Page 43: "There is much evidence . . .": Turner, "An Experimental Study of the Auditory Powers of the Giant Silkworm Moths," p. 332.

PICTURE CREDITS

ACKNOWLEDGMENTS

Special thanks to Elizabeth Hearne and Molly MacRae for their generous readings.

I am also grateful to Thomas Weissinger, African American Studies and Philosophy Bibliographer at the University of Illinois Library; the University of Illinois Library; Jill Hartke, Reference Specialist, the State Historical Society of Missouri; the Spencer Research Library, University of Kansas; and the Children's Department of the Champaign Public Library.

Calkins Creek
An imprint of Boyds Mills & Kane, a division of Astra Publishing House
calkinscreekbooks.com
Printed in China

ISBN: 978-1-62979-558-4
Library of Congress Control Number: 2018962348

First edition
10 9 8 7 6 5 4 3

Design by Barbara Grzeslo
The type is set in Neutraface.
The illustrations are digital.